The Kindness Paradigm

The Kindness Paradigm

Cheryl Jensen

Contact the author via email:

cconnerjensen@outlook.com

website: thekindnessparadigm.com

ISBN: 149736792
ISBN-13: 978-1497362796

ACKNOWLEDGMENTS

The author thanks His Holiness, the 14th Dalai Lama, for holding compassion for us until we are able to hold it for ourselves.

The author thanks Abraham-Hicks for defining the concepts of allowing and accepting, and for opening the conversation on vibration.

PREFACE

Each of us has a personal connection to the eternal source of all life. The Kindness Paradigm is the practical application of such eternal wisdom. It is the result of distilling the information I have received over the past ten years into a format for everyday use.

Cheryl Jensen
August 13, 2015

CONTENTS

INTRODUCTION

The basic premise of *The Kindness Paradigm* is that we need to develop a common vision for our world's future. Just as people make plans for vacation, deciding where to go and what to do, we need to make plans for our future. We need to decide together what we want for ourselves as individuals and as a world community. Then we need to determine how to achieve it.

The Kindness Paradigm is one such vision wherein we use kindness to develop the spiritual gifts inherent in each of us. The goal of the Kindness Paradigm is individual happiness and global harmony, achieved by creating an environment in which people flourish.

While there may be many viable ideas for our future, the author's hope for the Kindness Paradigm is simply to open conversation regarding a common vision for our future.

THE KINDNESS PARADIGM

The time has come to shift our social paradigm to one of kindness, in which universal happiness is the driving force behind our decisions. To establish a paradigm of kindness we must create a shared vision, one that enhances all lives and diminishes none. It must hold true for everyone.

A vision that holds true for everyone begins with commonalities. A vision that concludes with human flourishing does so through individual happiness.

The qualities that fulfill these requirements

are to feel a sense of safety and security that leaves one free to follow their interests and inspirations; to thrive; to prosper; to maintain relationships that are satisfying and fulfilling; and to reach the end of each day feeling satisfied and fulfilled.

The Kindness Paradigm holds that supporting all individuals in the pursuit of their interests and inspirations will unlock these qualities and unleash individual happiness and thus human flourishing. Indeed, it holds that such support is the only thing that will.

Additionally, the Kindness Paradigm holds kindness to be the primary tool for affecting this change.

KINDNESS

Kindness is an internal feeling of goodness. It is warmth of spirit that spills out of us as friendliness, generosity, and consideration of others. Kindness leads us to express a gentle, relaxed, friendly concern for one another and to be helpful. Kindness is inclusive.

Kindness helps us make decisions that support the happiness and well-being of ourselves and those around us. It is a by-product of compassion so the first step in establishing a paradigm of kindness is discovering how to experience compassion.

COMPASSION

Compassion is a sympathetic emotion that, like love, is defined by deep and abiding appreciation for all things. It is expansive and often produces a desire to uplift those who struggle. This deep and abiding appreciation is held for all things, including the way others live their lives and express themselves.

When we hold compassion for ourselves and for others, we radiate an aura of inclusiveness. In this encompassing safety we and those around us have the physical liberty to pursue our dreams as well as the emotional liberty to do so.

Emotions are intrinsic to mankind and each of us has the capacity to feel compassion. Many of us, however, do not know what compassion feels like. Emotions such as frustration, jealousy, anger, guilt, depression, and fear are resistant emotions. These negative emotions act as a wedge, blocking our ability to feel pleasant, positive emotions like compassion.

Holding onto negative emotions is unnatural and uncomfortable and requires work, the way it requires work to hold an inflated basketball underwater. Just as an inflated basketball springs to the surface when released, we instantly return to pleasant resting emotions such as peace and contentment when we release negative emotions. Peace and contentment are within an emotional spectrum that includes compassion. From resting emotions compassion becomes a viable option. This option does not exist when negative emotions are dominant.

RELAXING THE MIND

Relaxing the mind is the first step toward releasing negative emotions. Relaxing the mind helps us come to peace with whatever is occurring whether we agree with it or not.

Two methods for relaxing the mind are meditation and consciously letting go of judgment.

Meditation is an effective approach to relaxing the mind because it allows the mind to rest. It is a time when the mind has no work to do. In the Kindness Paradigm meditation is used to let go of thoughts and inner chatter. By doing so one is able to allow the mind to become still.

To consciously let go of judgment, one must maintain a level of self-awareness wherein one notices resistance within themselves when it arises. Resistance arises when a negative judgment is made. When one is aware of negative judgments one may consciously release them by letting go of the thought that produced the judgment. When thought is released this way the resistant emotion that accompanied the thought is also released.

Conscious letting go of judgment is a quick method that can be applied any time it is needed whereas meditation is preemptive.

ALLOWING

Allowing is the next step towards consistently feeling compassion. As Abraham-Hicks teaches, when we allow another person to live their life as they choose without encouraging them or expecting them or even hoping for them to be or act a certain way we are allowing. We willingly allow all things to exist because suppression promotes resistance and resistance is an emotion that blocks compassion.

Allowing is a scary concept for some because it means permitting things to exist that we do not like, agree with, or want in our lives.

The Kindness Paradigm, though, is about a planet full of individuals seeking personal fulfillment. Living in a paradigm of kindness is about choosing a life of kindness for oneself while simultaneously allowing every other individual the dignity to make their own choices, whatever they may be.

If allowing others to make different choices is frightening remember that the path to achieving an environment in which everyone flourishes is not through fear but through compassion.

To move beyond the fear of allowing others to make choices different from our own, consider what humans are. Humans are eternal beings inhabiting a body on a temporary basis; we are powerful extensions of a supreme creator; we are on Earth seeking growth. Our range of emotions stretches from shame, guilt and depression through hate and anger, past hope into love, peace, and harmony. Though our emotions stretch all the way to rapturous joy, our true essence rests in love, peace, and harmony.

Life is challenging and complex and it is sometimes difficult to allow others the freedom to be and do as they choose while maintaining our own restful emotions. We sometimes begin to feel powerless instead of powerful.

When the dark side of our nature is expressed, it is because we have become, due to the complex and difficult nature of life, out of balance with our eternal life source. When we become misaligned, we lose the flow of power from our life source. This is similar to the way the flow of water is blocked in a kinked hose.

This blockage is frightening. Getting enough of the life source flowing through us is just as important as getting enough oxygen. In the same way we would struggle to breathe if we needed more oxygen, we struggle to restore the flow of our life source. Struggling to regain that flow of life source looks like frustration, jealousy, anger, guilt, depression, and fear. These emotions appear in us, with their accompanying negative behaviors, when we misalign with our life source.

Allowing others to be and do as they choose is easier knowing that all action, no matter how inappropriate that action may seem, stems from an attempt to align with our life source and regain a sense of power.

DETACHING FROM OUTCOME

Detaching from outcome helps us become allowing. We are better able to detach from outcome when we realize that nothing exists that is truly good or bad. We feel positive about something or negative about it, but nothing is truly good or bad.

Positive and negative feelings are guidance, a sort of steering system the supreme creator designed for us. Each person is linked to this guidance individually and what feels positive to one may feel negative to another.

When positive emotion is experienced, we instinctively know to seek more of whatever caused it. Often, though, we don't know what to do with negative emotions.

The purpose of negative emotions is to notify us when we move out of alignment with our life source. They tell us we are steering in the wrong direction. The best way to approach negative emotion is to acknowledge the depth of feeling it creates. Grieve if needed, or be angry for a while, but as soon as is reasonably possible begin to seek the opposite of whatever created the negative emotion.

Opposites are solutions. Opposites feel powerful.

It is important to note that no one else must change for our solution to be effective. Others may participate if they choose, but a solution that requires someone else to participate is not a solution.

In the search for opposites, we find things that interest us and that are personally fulfilling. This leads to positive emotion. This is the reason we choose to live in the Earth environment where we are provided with such magnificent contrast. We learn what we like and what brings us happiness by bumping up against those things that cause emotional discomfort and then actively searching for their opposite, where we find contented fulfillment.

Knowing how to use 'bad' feelings to find pleasing outcomes is a powerful tool. This feeling of power makes it easier to detach from outcome and allow all things to exist whether we like them or not.

ACCEPTING

Once we release the fear of allowing others to follow their hearts' calling, even when it differs vastly from our own, we enter a second phase, the phase of accepting. Accepting means that we not only allow others to be as they are and do what they do, but we do so in a relaxed, warm, welcoming way.

Acceptance stems from the stirring of compassion created by allowing. Acceptance is more than allowing another to do as they please. Acceptance is feeling love for the choices of others regardless of how incomprehensible they may seem.

When we place our attention upon the violence and atrocities committed every day it can be difficult to feel loving towards the perpetrators. It is much easier to be accepting of other's actions when we understand we do what we do in an attempt to regain the inherent feeling of power that is all of our birthright.

When others take negative action in order to regain their sense of power it is easy to feel as though we could become victims of their actions. But there are no victims.

Humans have the power to repel negative outcome. We are designed to do so simply by consistently choosing the most positive thoughts we can find.

People attract and repel life experiences based on dominant emotions. Like a magnet that pushes from one side and pulls from the other, our emotions attract and repel life's events.

Emotions produce a vibrational harmonic. When a person experiences an event, they literally vibrate in harmonic resonance equal to their feelings about it. This resonance is attractive and pulls more similar events into their life.

This is true of all emotions. The power of this attractive resonance is equal to the intensity of the emotion.

When we feel positive emotions such as confidence, peace, or compassion we are magnets attracting positive life experiences while simultaneously repelling negative events. When we feel depressed, fearful, angry, or other negative emotions we are magnets attracting negative life events while simultaneously repelling positive events.

This is how we interact with, and participate with, our surroundings and this is why there are no victims. Knowing this, we are better able to accept the negative actions of others.

Adults can consciously choose to hold positive emotion thus repelling negative events, although not all adults know how to. Most babies and young children cannot actively hold positive emotion. As previously stated, when we hold compassion for ourselves and for others we radiate in an inclusive way. We provide emotional stability so those around us who may be unable to consistently hold their own positive emotions, have a stable emotional template to follow.

Understanding that life events are attracted by our own dominant emotions means that the actions of others are no longer a concern. Our primary concern now becomes our own happy contentment and that of those around us.

When we are able to lovingly accept the choices of others, whether we agree with those choices or not, we have attained compassion. When we are able to look at what is ugly or fearful and feel love pulsate within, we have attained compassion. Just as compassion stems from accepting, kindness is a natural result of compassion.

We harness kindness to temper our decision making. The happiness and well-being of our self and others is now the driving force behind our decisions. When a decision benefits everyone, including our neighbors, it is a good decision.

A natural extension of employing kindness this way is that we are able to gently nurture those around us.

REWRITING OUR VIEW OF NURTURING

The simple act of gently nurturing one another creates a sense of safety and security that helps each of us blossom into the person we intended to be when we planned this life.

Nurturing has come to mean a thing we do with babies and little children. By the time we reach adulthood it is somehow expected that we will not need 'that stuff' anymore; that to need nurturing is to be weak and to nurture is also weak.

The Kindness Paradigm hopes to rewrite this view of nurturing. The Kindness Paradigm uses Merriam-Webster's Online Dictionary definition to define nurture as helping (something or someone) to grow, develop, or succeed. In the Kindness Paradigm we seek to nurture every individual in a posture of supportive friendliness regardless of age, intellect, finances, state of health or level of likeability.

The Kindness Paradigm encourages such nurturing because it creates a sense of safety for those around us. Our minds are free to imagine. We feel free to follow inspiration and we are continually encouraged.

Within our current paradigm, when a person shows talent musically or athletically at an early age this young one's abilities are polished and developed. In the Kindness Paradigm those whose gifts are not so obviously marketable are also developed. For example, the person who only knows how to love well will have their gift nurtured the same way we nurture a budding tennis protégé or gymnast.

The Kindness Paradigm then extrapolates this to adults so that every person, without regard to age or apparent ability, is nurtured and encouraged in the pursuit of their interests and their inspirations.

WE HAVE INNATE TALENT

The Bible tells us we each are given at least one spiritual gift. A spiritual gift is something we are born with. It is innate within us, and we are instinctively drawn to it. The discovery of our gifts is stimulated by interest and inspiration.

We are drawn inexorably to explore our interests and inspirations because it feels good to do so. That is how our supreme creator gets us to develop and share our gifts: by giving us inspiration and then causing us to have emotions that feel good when we think about and act on that inspiration.

Furthermore, our skill sets are designed by our supreme creator to be complementary. As a social whole, we are incomplete because so many have not developed their gifts. In a social paradigm of kindness, it is the expectation of society that individuals will explore their interests fully. Not only for individual happiness, but for the collective good of the community. This exploration is nurtured in infinite ways.

WORK LIFE BECOMES LIFE'S WORK

Pursuing interests inevitably produces a prosperous livelihood. Just as a bird goes about doing what a bird does, making its livelihood by following its instincts, the human is designed to make a livelihood doing the thing it is instinctively drawn to do.

In essence, it is the continual unfolding of our talents that causes us to thrive and to prosper.

When we industriously go about doing things we enjoy we suddenly realize that work and life are the same. They are not separate. Life's work, in the Kindness Paradigm, means the work that gives one life. It is the reason for existence. This kind of work is animating. It gives meaning to life and adds to the fulfillment and satisfaction in each day.

The most important thing one will ever do for oneself and indeed for the whole of mankind is find the thing one wants to do and do it regardless of age, health, ability or even skill.

THE CHALLENGE

Living in a paradigm of kindness means that as individuals, and as a social whole, we look for answers that get to the root of our problems and implement those solutions with compassion and kindness. The challenge for us is to adequately cope with the immediate issues created by negative behaviors because sometimes there will be no good answer.

The only thing we can do in solving immediate issues is make the best choices we know how to make while simultaneously solving our primary issue. Most of us think that negative behavior is the primary issue. It isn't. Negative behavior is the result of our primary issue.

Our primary problem is that we become misaligned with our eternal life source and thus feel disempowered. Once this occurs, we do not know how to become realigned or even that it is an option to do so. Negative behavior is a direct result of feeling disempowered.

In a kindness paradigm it is our mission to make it easy for one another to realign with our individual sources of eternal power. We do that by finding our own compassion. We then radiate a steady, stable field of inclusivity that helps others feel safe around us and makes it easy for them to maintain a positive outlook. We treat others with kindness and understanding while they decide whether they want to find their compassion and realign with their personal source of power.

And from compassion, this powerful emotional home base, we firmly focus on what we want to see in the world and continually kindle even the smallest progress in that direction.

This is what will alleviate the need for negative behavior. This is what will solve our root problem of misalignment and bring answers to all other troubles.

Once our primary issue is resolved our other problems will fade away. They will fade away because we stop focusing on them and focus instead on what we do want.

ABOUT THOSE WHO DON'T WANT TO PARTICIPATE

For those who don't believe change is needed or who don't believe change is possible, how do we help them to want it? How do we help one another want to participate in this new vision? The answer is: We don't. All that is needed for success in shifting our current paradigm to one of kindness is for one person to want to make a change, followed by one more.

This shift is voluntary and undertaken one individual at a time. One by one we make a personal paradigm shift. Eventually, enough people will voluntarily subscribe to this idea that we will reach a tipping point. When that tipping point is reached the shift to kindness will fall into place in the natural order of things without regard to who has yet to agree.

THINGS WE MIGHT EXPECT TO SEE

The Kindness Paradigm is a reinvention of our global social system. The goal is human flourishing. In a paradigm of kindness, the happiness of individuals is more important than economics. If the Kindness Paradigm has a motto it is: Personal fulfillment for the benefit of all.

The first thing we are likely to notice as the shift to kindness occurs is that a shorter work week is crucial to individual well-being.

In a paradigm of kindness, the standard

workweek is 15-30 hours. A workday may be as short as two or three hours. We choose a shorter workday because it better reflects the way our minds and bodies work. Creativity runs dry and our bodies tire after a few hours. When this happens, we allow ourselves to rest and refill. Then we move on to the next segment of our day.

People live close to work, and it is pleasant to walk or bike to work. The reduced workweek leaves plenty of time for family and the activities of daily living, for socialization, play and entertainment.

Homes are built with comfort and ease in mind. They are self-sustaining and easy to maintain.

Construction is sound and development is both considered and considerate, exhibiting sensitivity for nature.

There is a resurgence of community evidenced by a rebirth of walkable neighborhoods. There are sidewalks, parking strips and bike lanes. Parks large and small dot our neighborhoods. Pets are welcome and wildlife peacefully co-exists with us.

Landscaping is creative and beautiful, satisfying the need for privacy, wildlife habitat and food.

Fresh, wholesome food is affordable and easily available.

The various means of transportation are safe, efficient, and pleasant.

We take pride in the work we choose and treat it like the gift it is. Work options are as varied as the individuals who do the work. Local craftsmen are sought after. Working from a home office or shop is common and the sole proprietor business is commonplace.

The arts are achievable, valued and varied.

Education is geared to the needs of the individual.

Laws are supportive.

We take interest in the well-being of our neighbors. There is a sense of being part of a world community, so we care for the well-being of our world neighbors as well as our next-door neighbors.

Compassion is held for those who transgress as well as for those who are transgressed against. When a person does need to make amends, their efforts are received with understanding.

In essence, a kindness paradigm fosters an

environment in which variety and harmony co-exist and our ability to imagine is the only limiting factor.

WRAPPING IT UP

There are five tenets the Kindness Paradigm holds to be true: Every individual needs to feel a sense of safety and security that leaves one free to follow their interests and inspirations; to thrive; to prosper; to maintain relationships that are satisfying and fulfilling; and to reach the end of each day feeling satisfied and fulfilled.

We achieve a feeling of safety and security by developing compassion. Compassion produces a positive energetic vibration that attracts positive life experiences. When we carry positive energy in the range of compassion we are no longer victims. There are no victims. Instead, we are powerful attractors of life experience.

When we hold compassion we are not critical, nor do we place blame. What we do is love well. We learn from compassion that love is not something that we get from others or give to others. Instead, love is what we are and when we hold that loving emotion dominant over other emotions we attract solid, satisfying relationships.

Compassion produces kindness. Kindness is used to nurture one another as we develop our gifts, and to temper decision making so that our decisions support our needs and the needs of our neighbors.

This does not mean we cater to others or define our lives by their needs. Each person is responsible for finding their own happiness.

Our job is simply to uplift those around us while pursuing our dreams.

In such a caring environment we are free emotionally as well as physically to follow our inspiration. We are drawn instinctively to activities that we are suited to. In the way a bird earns its living simply by doing what a bird does, humans are designed to instinctively pursue things that will provide them with a prosperous livelihood. Pursuing these interests and developing skill in performing them provides a sense of fulfillment and satisfaction. We feel good. We thrive.

When individuals thrive, communities thrive. When communities thrive, nations thrive. And when all the nations thrive we will have achieved our goal: Human flourishing.

ABOUT THE AUTHOR

Cheryl Jensen is the author of askhiggins.com, a metaphysically oriented advice column. She conducts cleansing meditations for earth, air, and water, especially after such events as oil spills or radiation leaks, and frequently conducts meditations designed to restore global harmony.

Contact Cheryl by email:

cconnerjensen@outlook.com